PRAISE FOR **REALLY REALLY**

"The terrific opening scene in itself justifies the advance buzz. *Really Really* is a take-no-prisoners indictment of the young men and women poised to inherit the earth . . . Mr. Colaizzo already possesses an assured appreciation of the addictive power of ambiguity, which he manipulates with a bait-and-switch mastery that never lets up . . . Morality is not a talking point here. This is *Lord of the Flies* with smartphones."
—Ben Brantley, *The New York Times*

"A crackling new play...sucks you in with its brio and caustic wit and holds you with its teasingly clever double-edged plot."
—Peter Marks, *The Washington Post*

"*Really Really* is . . . edgy, funny, caustic, shocking . . . brilliant."
—Sophie Gilbert, *Washingtonian*

"The playwright displays an undeniable gift for narrative with his gripping 'he said/she said' plotline . . . This provocative drama displays a crackling intensity."
—Frank Scheck, *The Hollywood Reporter*

"In Colaizzo's world, love is like a minefield of nasty negotiations . . . unassailably painful, erotic, and real."
—Hilton Als, *The New Yorker*

D0596033

PAUL DOWNS COLAIZZO's produced plays include *Really Really* and *Pride in the Falls of Autrey Mill*. He is currently writing for HBO.

REALLY REALLY

REALLY
REALLY

A PLAY BY

PAUL DOWNS COLAIZZO

OVERLOOK DUCKWORTH
NEW YORK • LONDON

First published in the United States and the United Kingdom in 2013 by
Overlook Duckworth, Peter Mayer Publishers, Inc.

NEW YORK
141 Wooster Street
New York, NY 10012
www.overlookpress.com
For bulk and special sales, please contact sales@overlookny.com,
or write us at the above address.

LONDON
30 Calvin Street
London E1 6NW
info@duckworth-publishers.co.uk
www.ducknet.co.uk
For bulk and special sales, please contact sales@duckworth-publishers.co.uk,
or write us at the above address.

Cataloging-in-Publication Data is available from the Library of Congress.
A catalogue record for this book is available from the British Library.

Book design and type formatting by Bernard Schleifer
Manufactured in the United States of America
ISBN 978-1-4683-0807-5 (US)
ISBN 978-0-7156-4744-8 (UK)
1 3 5 7 9 10 8 6 4 2

REALLY REALLY

PREFACE

Is it generational or just a period of life?

When I wrote *Really Really*, I was twenty-one years old,
and I truly believed that my generation was headed down
a very dangerous path—a group of people dipped in self-
centeredness and amoral choices, set only to advance
ourselves, creating a society of untrustworthy narcissists.
Now, I'm not so sure.

At twenty-eight, I'm more of an adult than I was when
I wrote this play, and I've noticed a shift in myself and my
peers in regard to our attitudes and outlooks on life and each
other. Namely, it feels like we're not as big of dicks to each
other as we used to be. Why is this? Maybe we just grew up.
Or maybe I was more sensitive seven years ago than I am
today. Or maybe now I've just surrounded myself with different
people who were never dicks to begin with.

Was this generation once terrible and now cured? It's
hard to say, since traits that are said to define all members of
a generation never truly account for everybody within that
group anyway. But what's easy to say is that our generation is
not all bad. And furthermore, we might not be all that different
from generations past.

In 2012, when the play premiered in Arlington, Virginia,
after five years of workshopping and rewriting the thing, I was

excited to present what I considered to be a cautionary tale for my generation, an exploration of our greed and lack of empathy. And in a way, that's exactly how the play was received. But I was surprised to find that the reactions of many older audience members were not ones of distaste or disappointment, but rather of nostalgia.

Standing in the lobby of the Signature Theatre after preview performances, I spoke to audience members about their individual experiences while watching the play. I was surprised to learn of the astonishing level of relatability to the twenty-one-year-old characters from people in their sixties and upwards. "That was us," a patron said to me. "We were like that too."

What were these audience members telling me? Are Millennials all that different from the generations that came before us? Or are we just going along the path that everyone else has already traveled?

A new study, recently published in *Developmental Psychology*, shows that most teenage brains actually lack a strong ability to experience empathy, and that this has nothing to do with parenting, and everything to do with the way our minds are naturally wired. This idea should come as no surprise to anyone who has ever attended high school or watched a movie that takes place in that prison/torture experiment that puts nerds and cheerleaders side-by-side. But what it does illuminate is that this idea of the selfish, horrible Millennial is a misnomer, and that the fend-for-yourself mentality that many people in college and in their early twenties espouse is just part of life.

Really Really explores that period of life. Specifically, it's a play that explores a group of people still in this period of development, and going through it during one of the greatest economic crises in American history. It's a play about people who were promised a world of endless opportunity and, just as that promise was set to be delivered, instead experience a threat to their once-privileged futures. With very few jobs and very little security, in order to continue chasing his or her American dream, each student must focus on what they want, first and foremost, all while being told by experts that they are terrible people. Everything hits at once. *Really Really* is about a group of winners who feel the threat of losing for the very first time.

PAUL DOWNS COLAIZZO
December 2013

Really Really had its world premiere at Signature Theatre, Arlington, Virginia, February 2012. Artistic Director: Eric Schaeffer, Managing Director: Maggie Boland.

Directed by Matthew Gardiner, Scenic Design by Misha Kachman, Costume Design by Kathleen Geldard, Lighting Design Colin K. Bills, Sound Design by Matt Rowe, Fight Director Casey Kaleba, New York Casting Stuart Howard & Paul Hardt, Production Stage Manager Julie Meyer.

CAST:

COOPER	Evan Casey
GRACE	Lauren Culpepper
JIMMY	Danny Gavigan
JOHNSON	Paul James
LEIGH	Bethany Anne Lind
DAVIS	Jake Odmark
HALEY	Kim Rosen

Really Really had its New York premiere at MCC Theater 2012. Artistic Directors: Robert LuPone, Bernard Telsey, and William Cantler, Executive Director: Blake West.

Directed by David Cromer, Sound Design and Original Composition by Daniel Kluger, Scenic Design by David Korins, Costume Design by Sarah Laux, Lighting Design by David Weiner.

CAST:

COOPER	David Hull
GRACE	Lauren Culpepper
JIMMY	Evan Jonigkeit
JOHNSON	Kobi Libii
LEIGH	Zosia Mamet
DAVIS	Matt Lauria
HALEY	Aleque Reid

ACT I – A Sunday in Spring

Scene 1 – The Girls' Apartment

Scene 2 – The Guys' House

Scene 3 – The Girls' Apartment

Scene 4 – They Guys' House

Scene 5 – The Future Leaders of America Conference

Scene 6 – The Girls' Apartment

Scene 7 – The Guys' House

ACT II – Monday

Scene 1 – The Future Leaders of America Conference

Scene 2 – The Girls' Apartment

Scene 3 – The Guys' House

Scene 4 – A Laundromat

Scene 5 – The Guys' House

Scene 6 – The Girls' Apartment

Scene 7 – The Guys' House

Scene 8 – The Girls' Apartment, The Theater

ACT I

SCENE 1

Lights up on a college apartment. It is big, mildly messy, and clearly inhabited by women. The girls who live there have tried to decorate the place many times without finishing before they begin REDECO-RATING. It is dark outside.

As the pre-show music continues to play full blast, the front door swings open, silencing the music. The two girls that live in this apartment stand outside for a moment before they enter. They are drunk and laughing so hard that you would think that they were high.

GRACE is tall and beautiful. Her hand is bleeding and her attempts to stop the blood are failing.

LEIGH is beautiful in her own right. She is not standing up straight.

They still stand there. Laughing. And laughing.

GRACE enters the apartment, drops her bag, aiming for the kitchen counter but mis-launching it to the floor. She undresses as she pours herself a full glass of water and drinks the whole thing. She has given up and is leaving blood drops everywhere she goes.

LEIGH, after a few too many moments, walks into the apartment and slams the door. She stands motionless before heading to the couch and looking for her cell phone. She finds it. It's a flip phone. She looks to see if she got a text message. Nope. She closes it and sets it down. She picks it back up and looks at it.

She opens the phone. She holds down a button, then puts it on speaker mode.

VOICEMAIL LADY (*From the phone.*)   There are no new messages in your mailbox.

LEIGH *closes the phone. She opens it, holding the button.*

VOICEMAIL LADY (*From the phone.*)   There are no new messages in your mailbox.

She closes the phone. She opens it, holding the button..

VOICEMAIL LADY (*From the phone.*)   There are no new messages in your mailbox.

GRACE, *now in her underwear, turns off all the lights as she exits toward her bedroom.*

LEIGH *crosses upstage to the bathroom, turns on the light and starts the shower. She is walking with caution. She walks back to her cell phone. She holds the button.*

VOICEMAIL LADY (*From the phone.*)   There are no new messages in your mailbox.

LEIGH *picks up a sweatshirt from the floor and puts it on over her clothes. She sits down on the couch facing outward. She is working to breathe. Her eyes well up. She is motionless.*

LEIGH Ow.

SCENE 2

A house on a college campus. The play is clearly inhabited by college men who come from money. The house is typically clean but the remnants from the party the night before are still contaminating the room. JOHNSON *is dressed for the day and playing a racing game on Xbox.* COOPER *is standing in the doorway to his bedroom and is half asleep and angry. Immediately on lights up—*

COOPER *(Eyes almost closed, as loud as a soldier.)* Johnson, what the fuck are you doing?!

JOHNSON What?

COOPER What the fuck are you—

JOHNSON I'm playing the—

COOPER It's 8:15!

JOHNSON You told me I could come over here and play the—

COOPER In the morning!

JOHNSON *(To the game.)* OH!

COOPER You're yelling!

JOHNSON *(Still at the game.)* FUCK!

COOPER I was sleeping. Davis is sleeping. We were drinking all night and you are yelling!

JOHNSON *You're* yelling!

COOPER I fucking live here!

JOHNSON Oh so your voice is special? Just 'cause you live here your voice doesn't go through the walls?

COOPER JESUS CHRIST, JOHNSON!

JOHNSON I'm taking a break. Shouldn't you be up anyway? Don't you have to study for midterms?

COOPER I don't have any midterms.

JOHNSON None?!

COOPER Nope!

JOHNSON Ugh. That makes me so jel.

COOPER What? Jel?

JOHNSON What? Jel? Jel! It means "jealous." How do you not know that?

COOPER You sound like a douche.

COOPER *gets a text.*

JOHNSON Well I think it's cool, so, like—

COOPER Oh yeah. Shit.

JOHNSON Who's that?

COOPER Jenny Abrahamson. She lost her tooth here last night.

JOHNSON A tooth?

COOPER It's really her fault though. We had bottle openers everywhere.

JOHNSON She's hot.

COOPER She's fat.

JOHNSON She's hot fat.

COOPER What the fuck is wrong with you, man? You leave our party—our once-a-year, Tunnel of Love—

JOHNSON I made you a cake!

COOPER —to get a good night's sleep, and then you bring your tiny dick over to my house to play your outdated tiny dick video games?!

JOHNSON Sorry.

COOPER At 8:15 in the morning?!

JOHNSON I don't need your stupid party to get laid. I get laid all year.

COOPER GO HOME!

JOHNSON Everyone deserves some time off, Cooper!

COOPER Not at my *house*!

JOHNSON Oh I'm sorry. This visit is sending your day planner into a big fucking tailspin.

COOPER I've got shit to do.

JOHNSON What shit?

COOPER I do things.

JOHNSON Name three.

COOPER How about three things I didn't do: Didn't make a cake. Didn't wake up early to play video games. Didn't suck a dick somewhere in the in-between.

JOHNSON You are totes pussy jel.

COOPER What?

JOHNSON It's self-explanatory, Cooper!

COOPER (*To the video game.*) LOOK OUT!

JOHNSON Fuck! No! I knew it. I knew he was going to take me out.

COOPER Keep your eyes on the horizon. That's the first rule.

JOHNSON I hate my life.

JOHNSON *puts down his controller in anger.*

COOPER Hey—Good old Davis got laid last night.

JOHNSON No.

COOPER Yes.

JOHNSON *immediately turns off the video game and pays* COOPER *his full attention.*

They are both nodding. No one is talking.

JOHNSON So—go ahead—

COOPER Who me? Fucking me? The guy who you think doesn't do anything?

JOHNSON Ok—I'm sorry—you're very busy. It's gotta be hard to look for a job that's already waiting in your father's hand.

COOPER Fuck you. Suck my balls.

JOHNSON I'm not being derisive.

COOPER Suck my balls and say I'm king. Derisive? Fuck you.

JOHNSON You know what? It doesn't even matter who he slept with. I'm just glad he got some this year. I never liked Natalie.

COOPER I'm king!

JOHNSON He should be focusing on graduation. He's too nice to be sludging around like a pathetic heartbroken tool bag. If you had an ounce of the sophistication that Davis has then you might get laid every once in awhile too.

COOPER I get laid.

JOHNSON Name one.

COOPER You don't know everything!

JOHNSON Fine by me. I get laid.

A bedroom door opens and a very hung-over DAVIS *enters.*

JOHNSON Who'd you bone? Tell me quickly! Who'd you bone?

COOPER *tackles* JOHNSON *to the floor.*

JOHNSON NO! UNCLE! UNCLE! DUDE!

COOPER I'm the motherfucking king! Say it!

JOHNSON DUDE! GET OFF! UNCLE!

COOPER Davis—you say a word I will use your balls for tennis.

DAVIS Good morning?

JOHNSON *bites* COOPER.

COOPER (*Screaming.*) AHHHHHHH! WEIRDO! YOU WEIRDO!

JOHNSON *pulls* COOPER*'s hair as he locks down on his bite.*

COOPER LEIGH! He slept with Leigh you fucking girl!

JOHNSON *releases.*

JOHNSON No way!

COOPER Jesus!

JOHNSON No fucking way!

COOPER You cunt!

JOHNSON (*To* DAVIS.) You dirty! You dirty dirty!

DAVIS You're screaming.

JOHNSON Mum's the word, Davis. I promise. This is your day, kinda.

COOPER Johnson I am going to plug your ass with blades so we can all identify the dudes you are fucking!

JOHNSON Maria, Grace, Jessie, Tiffany. So what now? I have eighteen minutes. You want to go to the lawn?

COOPER Yeah. I'll get my Frisbee. You coming, Davis? Or you need to throw up a little first?

JOHNSON I can't believe you're back in the game.

DAVIS What?

JOHNSON Does Grace know? Does the Jimster know? Oh fuck— am I an accomplice?

DAVIS Know what?

COOPER Yeah you and half the block. What kind of kinky shit were you doing in there, Davis?

DAVIS What are you talking about?

COOPER Did a trumpet start playing? Did she give you a check? That's what normally happens when you're the thousandth customer.

JOHNSON So how'd it happen? Start from the top.

COOPER Hey. It's none of our business what happened in there.

DAVIS What happened in where?

COOPER Cut it, Davis. I had my ear pressed against the door for the first five minutes.

JOHNSON Pussy Jel.

DAVIS Oh Leigh? Jimmy's Leigh?

JOHNSON Oh yeah—we are talking about Jimmy's Leigh, right?

COOPER No one is judging you. We're just glad you got laid and finally got over Natalie. This is step one. The next step is to get you to sleep with a girl who is cleaner than E. coli.

JOHNSON Cooper. Don't be a dick.

COOPER What? He fucked her. It's not like they're friends. Besides—she was probably the man in the sack anyway. Right, Davis?

DAVIS Ummm . . .

COOPER I mean no offense, Davis, you're my buddy but you're more of a Vice-President.

DAVIS Oh come on. That's bullshit. What the hell did I drink?

COOPER What didn't you drink? Your pants were down and your hopes were up about an hour before you even went into the bedroom.

DAVIS Who was here?

COOPER When?

DAVIS Last night.

JOHNSON At what point?

DAVIS The party. Who was here during the party?

COOPER After you went into your bedroom? After a while it pretty much started to clear out. Grace came back for Leigh but by that time the team had all left.

JOHNSON Motherfucking Grace. She's good peeps.

DAVIS Oh Jesus.

COOPER What all do you remember?

DAVIS I remember the keg coming.

COOPER Yeah?

DAVIS And Johnson leaving.

COOPER And nothing else besides your tongue bath with Leigh?

DAVIS OK, I have to go study.

JOHNSON You're telling me. Societal Animals midterm tomorrow.

DAVIS I have to get a B minus or higher.

COOPER Davis here is trying to graduate Magnum Cum Lady.

JOHNSON That's not how you say it. I'll help you study? I made index cards.

COOPER On pink paper with flowers.

JOHNSON On bright futures with dollar signs.

COOPER (*Mockingly.*) Oh is that right?

JOHNSON (*Mockingly.*) Yeah that's right.

COOPER (*Mockingly.*) Oh, ok.

JOHNSON *exits.*

COOPER So, you good?

DAVIS I just need some coffee and a shower and I'll be fine.

COOPER Right. I mean about Leigh. Feel good to get out there again?

DAVIS Oh. Yeah. I guess. Do we have any pizza left?

COOPER 'Cause listen—man to man—I think you really deserve to be happy.

That's awkward.

DAVIS Thanks man.

COOPER So—spill it—did you make her scream like she didn't want it?

DAVIS I don't wanna talk about it. I have to figure out what I'm going to say to Jimmy.

COOPER Don't say anything. Jim is a pansy, dude. He's useless in every scrum and then he third halfs like he owns the game.

DAVIS Aw, come on. He's just showing off for his dad.

COOPER Umm, his dad is pretty smart. He's on the fucking board. His son blows and he knows it.

DAVIS Alright if you'll excuse me, I have to put all of this on the back burner so that I can pass my exam, graduate college, fight for a good job, or any job, marry a lovely woman and assemble some sort of life.

COOPER Is that what you want?

DAVIS Oh I don't know.

COOPER You can't get what you want unless you know what you want.

DAVIS I want you to shut up so I can study.

COOPER Tests don't matter, Davis, I'm telling you.

DAVIS Oh really?

COOPER We're playing a totally different game than our parents did. You need to learn actual survival things, man. Stop working hard, you idiot. Work smart. Can you do that?

DAVIS Cooper?

COOPER Yeah?

DAVIS You know me. I can do anything.

SCENE 3

Back to the girls' apartment. It is the same day, mid-morning. GRACE *is making pancakes, listening to the news, and dressed for church. Her once bloody hand is now bandaged.*

A bedroom door opens and LEIGH *enters, wearing long sleeves and pants.*

GRACE Hey Mess. I made you coffee. And pancakes. I made too many so I hope you're hungry. My rent check is on the fridge and my Statistics midterm is right here in this folder. And I bought an air horn, since you'll be here alone for the next few days, that I'm keeping on the shelf. It says "Not for indoor use" but if you need to use it then you use it indoors, outdoors, on tours and through the floors, you understand me?

LEIGH Huh?

LEIGH *sits on the couch, reading a* Better Homes and Gardens *magazine with post-its sticking out of it.*

GRACE Grace to Leigh. Wake up. Also—I just want you to know—we all pitched in to get Jennie Abrahamson that dress she won't shut up about for her birthday. I took care of your contribution, don't worry—you don't have to pay me back. I told everyone it was from you. But you have to sign the card.

LEIGH I can pay you back.

GRACE Hell no! That's sweet and cute and kind but you're . . .

I mean—I got it. You can't go throwin' around money for designer dresses that you're not even going to wear.

LEIGH You don't have to do that. (*Genuinely.*) You look pretty. I like your hair.

GRACE Really? I feel like I look horrible.

LEIGH You don't. You look good. When are you leaving?

GRACE Now, honey. I have to make it to church before I leave for the conference. And I built in an extra twenty minutes so that I can drive my car with this useless flirp of a hand.

LEIGH Oh my God I totally forgot about that.

GRACE Apparently I did too. It must have bled until my alarm clock went off because my 1200-count white sheets are now gross hundred count blood red.

LEIGH Oh my God—you're immobile. You're handicapped now. You could probably get affirmative action points for that thing. Are you going to drop these off before you leave?

GRACE No I don't have time. How'd you sleep? Pleasantly, I assume?

LEIGH Ugh.

GRACE Oh God. There's blood on your shirt. How the hell did that happen?

LEIGH I didn't want to sleep alone. We cuddled for a little.

LEIGH *changes shirts.*

GRACE You WERE in my bed. Oh thank God. I thought maybe I had dreamt that and was discovering a lesbian side of myself. Did I bleed on you a lot?

LEIGH Do you need to go to the hospital?

GRACE I'm fine, I'm fine. It'll just be a little awkward shaking hands with my fellow Future Leaders of America. "Hi—I'm Grace. What happened to my hand? Oh I was drunk last night on my way home from a kegger and I tripped and fell over my slutty heels into a pile of broken glass by the dumpster where I was helping myself to some uneaten pizza while I waited for my roommate to finish up cheating on her boyfriend with a guy she's had a crush on since freshman year. Why won't you touch me?"

LEIGH You were waiting?

GRACE Don't mention it. That boy is hot, ok? He's the perfect man. Half the people at church right now are probably going to worship *him*.

LEIGH Yeah, but Grace—

GRACE No buts. I saw how you were looking at him all night. You were a freaking lioness on the prowl. And if I couldn't leap on top of him I wanted you to. I bet he is one hundred percent pure delicious.

LEIGH Huh.

GRACE Now you just have to let Jimmy down easy. It's about time you let that slug go.

LEIGH Tsk. Jimmy.

GRACE Out of sight, out of mind, and soon enough for you, out of your life.

LEIGH Be nice. Don't say anything.

GRACE You're an idiot. We only got home six hours ago. Why are you up?

LEIGH I couldn't sleep.

GRACE Were you staring at the ceiling, reliving the night, waiting to tell me every little detail?

LEIGH Oh, Grace.

GRACE Because that's exactly what I want to hear and I want to hear it right now.

LEIGH I don't want to.

GRACE Johnson won't touch me with midterms coming up. He calls me the fruit of temptation. LET A GIRL LIVE THROUGH YOU, OK?!

LEIGH You don't want to hear it.

GRACE But he's Davis. (*Beat.*)

LEIGH How do you not have a hangover?

GRACE Advil. Is this really happening? Are you not going to tell me about your night? (*Beat.*) You see this? This thing I used to call a hand? This is covered like a Muslim woman because it fought in the battle of Covering Your Ass. There are pancakes in the kitchen, an air horn on the shelf, and a manageable ounce of curiosity stirring in my sexually deprived yet ever-so-deserving soul. So, Leigh, the day has come—I am in the street, dying of thirst. Spit, Leigh. Spit into my mouth!

LEIGH Ok. Jesus.

GRACE But do the Cliff's Notes because I'm late.

LEIGH Well we went into the bedroom and—oh God I slept with my contacts in.

GRACE (*Referring to her hand.*)   MUSLIM WOMAN!

LEIGH   Look, Grace, it's my business, ok? You can feel as entitled as you want but when you take a minute to think about it, it is my business!

GRACE   Ok. Chill out.

LEIGH   I didn't ask for you to wait for me. I'm not a poor defenseless girl. If you wanted to actually save me, you wouldn't have let me go in with him, no matter how I was looking at him.

GRACE   Last night you thanked me.

LEIGH   Last night I couldn't walk home.

GRACE   You followed him into the bedroom.

LEIGH   Well Jesus—what a bad person I must be. If I had known all along that I was in control of everything, I wouldn't have made myself into such a fuck up! Such a worthless, deserving fuck up.

GRACE   Whoa whoa whoa, honey. Breathe. I'm sorry. You're right. I don't deserve to know anything. Look I gotta go but I love you, OK? You know that. I'll call you when I get to the hotel.

LEIGH   I made a mistake.

GRACE   We all make mistakes. You just made the hottest mistake on campus. Take it easy today.

There is a knock at the door. The door opens. JIMMY *stands in the doorway.*

JIMMY   Honey? (*Beat.*)

GRACE   I'm late. I'm late. I'm so late.

JIMMY Are you off the pill too?

GRACE Jimmy. I missed you. I'm not being sarcastic right now at all.

JIMMY Where are you off to?

GRACE Sainthood. (*Then to* LEIGH) Goodbye, Lover. Take a bath or something. That's actually my advice to you too, Jimmy.

GRACE *exits.*

JIMMY How's my baby?

LEIGH Oh good. I'm tired, but that's part of it all, I guess.

JIMMY (*To her stomach.*) And how's my baby baby?

LEIGH Kicking and probably screaming if she's anything like your mother.

JIMMY Hey no fair. Boys kick too.

LEIGH Wishful thinking. Do you want some pancakes?

JIMMY Totally. I'm starving. I missed you. A lot.

LEIGH Oh, baby.

JIMMY Did you miss me?

LEIGH Of course, baby.

JIMMY Did you tell Grace yet about the situation in the womb?

LEIGH No. Not yet. I don't want her to get all Jesus freak on me, you know?

JIMMY Jesus freak?

LEIGH Oh whatever.

JIMMY Did you make these?

LEIGH Do you like them?

JIMMY They're amazing.

LEIGH That's all that matters.

JIMMY So what'd you do while I was gone? (*Beat.*) Babe?

LEIGH Yeah?

JIMMY Are you feeling ok? You seem funny.

LEIGH Oh—I probably just have a lot on my mind. Midterms and stuff.

JIMMY Oh. Alright.

LEIGH But—why didn't you call?

JIMMY My phone died.

LEIGH I kind of needed to talk.

JIMMY Do you want to talk now?

LEIGH No. I'll get over it.

JIMMY Babe—is this your coffee? Caffeine, babe.

LEIGH No way. Are you kidding? It's Grace's.

JIMMY Two cups.

LEIGH I swear to God—she poured me a cup and I didn't have any. She leaves me so many dishes.

JIMMY That girl is something else.

LEIGH She's alright. She's good to me.

JIMMY Really? You can't even tell her that you've got a bun in the oven and she's supposed to be your best friend.

LEIGH Oh that's different.

JIMMY No. It's not.

LEIGH Look, she's good to me, ok?

JIMMY Uh—she's a bitch.

LEIGH She's just kidding with you. You know that.

JIMMY Sure. Yeah. But I'm just saying that, like, after you and I move in together, you know you're going to have to stop being friends with her.

LEIGH Blah blah.

JIMMY No babe, I mean it. I always learned not to allow people you don't like or don't trust into your home and I'm sorry but that girl is not welcome in any space that I pay for.

LEIGH But babe—it's my space too . . .

JIMMY Sacrifices, Leigh. We do what's best for each other. For example, I went on vacation with my family to the beach house this weekend. I came home a day early to be with you. (*Beat.*)

LEIGH Ok.

JIMMY And like right now. The whole team is at Rafter's eating wings and drinking mid-morning beers and where am I?

LEIGH Right here.

JIMMY That's right. With my lady and our baby. Sometimes God sends us forks in the road and we learn to love the view on the detour.

LEIGH Is that therapy something you think you're gonna stick with?

JIMMY We may have been on shaky ground before this, but knowing that you will have my kid . . .

LEIGH I know. It's amazing. I can't wait for him to be here.

JIMMY Aww . . . No more little girl? You changing your tune?

LEIGH When should we start looking at houses?

SCENE 4

Back to the boys' house.

DAVIS *is studying. He is deep in it.* COOPER *enters.*

COOPER DAVIS YOU PUSSY! You should have come to Rafter's. Steve's MILF was there. She paid the tab. How's it going?

DAVIS (*Reading from his book.*) "After copulation, the female praying mantis then bites off the head of the male mate. This decapitation speeds up the ejaculation process."

COOPER Ugh. Women.

DAVIS (*Still reading.*) "This mating ritual, despite popular belief, occurs less than 31 percent of the time. The female is more likely to eat the male if it is imminent to her survival. This process is referred to as "Sexual Cannibalism.""

COOPER I read in my Psych book last year that babies gnaw on your finger because they love you so much that they just want to eat you.

DAVIS Ugh—I'm never going to remember all of this stuff. It doesn't even relate to my major. I thought it'd be fun to take this class and now I think it'd be just as fun to move back in with my parents.

COOPER HEY! WE DON'T TALK LIKE THAT IN THIS HOUSE!

DAVIS Sometimes I really just want a way out of all of this. And why the hell are you not stressing?

COOPER What?

DAVIS Midterms. What's your deal?

COOPER I'm not in Societal Animals.

DAVIS Well Psych or whatever the hell else.

COOPER Aww, you know, I'm taking my time . . .

DAVIS When's your midterm?

COOPER No, no. I mean this "college lasts four years" thing. That was just a number some asshole picked out of thin air, you know? I'm young. I got time.

DAVIS I hate you.

COOPER It's like—I could stress out in my early twenties, and get work done and get that assignment in and write down what the professor says, but for what? To go work with my dad in this crazy market? That doesn't sound like fun to me! So—what? What's left? Option One—Pull a Davis. Stress about what you're told to do and force an early life heart attack on yourself. Not judging, just saying. And there's Option Two: The Cooper way. Four years? Hell no. Five. Six. Six and a half.

DAVIS That's not even allowed.

COOPER I know people. And this way, I end up saving time. Why? Because people who opted for Option One work towards retirement, but the blood pressure and the anxiety and the extra bullshit stress decrease the chance of that 401K seeing the light of day. So us Option Two guys—we'll cry at your funeral and mutter something about you being too young to die, but those extra three years I took in college, they turn into twenty or forty extra years added to my vacation called "life." You want a beer?

DAVIS You have bad parents.

COOPER I'm doing just fine.

DAVIS Yeah well in three months some of us have to find a job and then keep working because we won't get an automatic promotion when Daddy dies.

COOPER Hey glass house, you better put down those stones.

DAVIS No. No. Two totally different boats.

COOPER Like you're not well off.

DAVIS I have it just the opposite way.

COOPER Yeah?

DAVIS I have a name to uphold. Not a kingdom to take over.

COOPER Your dad is a CFO!

DAVIS He's never helped me at all! And my mom is a philanthropist. Professionally. And she already thinks she's spoiled me. If you think I'm seeing any of that money, you're a fucking moron.

COOPER Do you want to live that life you keep talking about?

DAVIS I don't know! Shut up! I want to pass this test!

COOPER Then you better study.

DAVIS I can't. I get a semi every time I read something about those fucked up mating rituals.

COOPER Ooo—So the ground hog didn't run away when it saw the light of day? I'm talking about your penis.

DAVIS Oh. I don't know. (*Beat.*) Can I say something that sounds gay?

COOPER Won't be the first time.

DAVIS Seriously—

COOPER Yes.

DAVIS I feel like—after last night I guess—whatever last night was—
I feel like . . .

COOPER Horny?

DAVIS No. Like, ready. I can't explain it. I feel like . . . I don't know
. . . like I have power again. And I want to be touched.

COOPER You didn't mean gay, like, you are trying to be gay with me,
did you?

DAVIS No—Fuck Cooper—No. I'm trying to be vulnerable here. I'm
just trying to get you to say you know what I mean and you know
the feeling.

COOPER Of wanting to get laid?

DAVIS Forget it.

COOPER No no—of like—wanting to be touched.

DAVIS I feel like—I don't know like—open. Like there's this new
space or something. Like—in my lungs. Like not nervous, but like,
you know what I mean?

COOPER Oh. Maybe.

DAVIS I don't want to Option One alone.

COOPER Well today's a good day then.

DAVIS Oh yeah?

COOPER Don't you see? Now you know that you hate your life.

DAVIS (*Sarcastically.*) Yeah. You're right. Today's great.

COOPER Look, Davis. You're the nicest guy I know—and I mean that in a completely negative way.

DAVIS Help me here, buddy.

COOPER Take control of one fucking thing.

DAVIS I'm trying to study.

COOPER That's what someone else wants you to do. What the fuck do you want?

DAVIS I don't need a fucking coach right now. I need a friend.

COOPER Fine! Ok, so—ah—give me a hug.

DAVIS No, Cooper, I'm OK.

COOPER No really, come here.

DAVIS I have to study.

COOPER Give me a fucking hug, dude.

DAVIS I don't want a hug.

COOPER Maybe I want a hug you cunt licker.

DAVIS Why the hell do you want a hug?

COOPER 'Cause you're my friend!

DAVIS No shit—we don't need to hug about it.

COOPER I'm not putting my fucking arms down until you give me a hug.

DAVIS You're a girl.

COOPER Hey—you said some pretty gay shit to me earlier about wanting to be touched and a new space up your ass.

DAVIS In my lungs.

COOPER I heard up your ass and I have a blog.

DAVIS Let me study.

COOPER Hug me!

DAVIS Oh my God!

DAVIS *hugs* COOPER. *After* DAVIS *gives in, it is a rather comforting, long hug.*

JOHNSON *enters. And stares.*

COOPER Johnson, I fucked your mother.

JOHNSON I know. She told me she couldn't feel a thing. Get far on the Societal Animals, Davis?

DAVIS What do I care about these crazy female cannibals?

COOPER This coming from the guy who was chewed up and spit out by a gorilla named Natalie.

JOHNSON I have note cards, notes, and I highlit . . . Highlighted. Sorry. I highlighted everything in the textbook that he mentioned in class.

COOPER There's also Option Three, which is the Total Fucking Loser Option.

DAVIS Cooper, play nice.

COOPER I don't wanna.

JOHNSON I want to order food before Jimmy comes. He never rounds up for tax and tip. Never. I'm not kidding. Literally never.

DAVIS Jimmy comes where?

JOHNSON I told him he could study with us.

DAVIS   What? Are you kidding me?

COOPER   Oh shit.

JOHNSON   What? Cooper—I thought you said . . .

COOPER   You're an idiot.

JOHNSON   Sorry. You're going to see him at practice tomorrow anyway.

DAVIS   I can avoid him at practice. Fuck, dude.

JOHNSON   Sorry. Well you shouldn't have screwed his girlfriend. That's not my fault.

DAVIS   Well what the hell am I supposed to do about it now?

JOHNSON   Maybe he won't come.

JIMMY *enters through the front door. Beat.*

COOPER   (*Fake thrilled.*) Jim/my!

JOHNSON   JIMMY!

DAVIS   Jim!

JIMMY   (*Feeding off of their excitement.*) HEY! HEYYY! HEEEEEYYYYYYY!

COOPER   Welcome back!

DAVIS   Yeah!

COOPER   How was your trip?

JIMMY   That fucking beach is killer. Nothing but sand and food and stars.

COOPER   And women, right?

JIMMY   I don't know what factory those women pop out of but fuckin A are they hot.

COOPER   Yeah? You tap any? We won't tell.

Beat, as they all anxiously stare at him awaiting his answer.

JIMMY Naw man. I'm committed. I'll let myself look, but anymore is no more.

COOPER Christian therapy? Really?

DAVIS Good for you. Look, Jimmy—bad news. I have to run, I just got a call from the library and I've gotta go. But—I'll see you tomorrow, yeah? Have fun studying and guys—have such a great time studying ok? There's beer in the fridge.

JIMMY Aww bummer. Well I'll see you later m—

DAVIS *exits.*

JIMMY Alright. Peace.

JOHNSON OK. I'm going to have to change the setup of the study game if it's just going to be the two of us. Unless, Cooper, you want to join.

COOPER I thought you'd never . . . Have you been reading my journal?

JIMMY You guys are funny together.

COOPER Beats being funny alone, Jimmy.

JOHNSON Studying.

COOPER Let's do something.

JOHNSON We are doing something.

COOPER Let's play a game or something.

JOHNSON We are on a schedule!

JIMMY What kind of game?

COOPER Something with a ball. Johnson loves balls.

JOHNSON Pussy jel. Pussy jel.

JIMMY What's Pussy Gel? Like KY?

JOHNSON Oh. No. It's like. Sometimes when people are going to use the word "jealous" they say jel instead.

COOPER Isn't that cute?

JIMMY Delicious.

JOHNSON Don't you have to study for something, Cooper? Like Intro to Being Dumb? Oh—Well you're actually probably doing really well in that one.

COOPER Uh. Oooh. Oof. Really rough go at that one, Johnson.

JOHNSON What is your GPA? Like how are you still on the team?

COOPER Are you kidding? First of all, they need the players and we can all agree on one thing: I am vicious. And second of all, my course load is minimal.

JIMMY Thanks to me.

COOPER Thanks to he.

JOHNSON I thought the rule . . .

COOPER Fuck rules. Jimmy's dad is the shit. He understands brotherhood. Pull a few strings . . .

JIMMY Anything for a buddy.

JOHNSON And what?

COOPER And, well . . .

JIMMY Just tell him. It's cool.

COOPER And I get to stay in school as long as I damn well please.

JIMMY Unless, you know, he kills my mother or something.

JOHNSON If you're not taking classes, you're not in school. You're just living on campus. And not even your campus. Just some campus. That's like maybe at the top of the most depressing things I've ever heard ever.

COOPER And I love it. Now which ball game will it be, kiddies?

JOHNSON We have to study, Cooper.

JIMMY Hey Cooper, did you ever put Gold Bond on your balls?

COOPER You know, I haven't. But I've always wanted to.

JIMMY I did it once in high school and it was fucking awesome.

COOPER You know what? I think I have some.

JOHNSON It's like I am the only person on Earth who wants a good future.

COOPER (*Retrieving the Gold Bond from the drawer.*) Here it is. Dump away.

JIMMY Here.

COOPER Johnson? You wanna try?

JOHNSON (*Buried in his book.*) That does not deserve a response.

COOPER I cannot wait to feel this glory.

JIMMY Good purchase, Coop.

COOPER This is actually Davis's.

JIMMY Steal it.

COOPER He'll probably just let me have it if I ask him. He's, um, really good at sharing. Right, Johnson?

JOHNSON Umm . . . yeah.

COOPER He shares everyone—thing. Sorry—I said one but I meant thing.

JOHNSON Are you kidding me with that?

COOPER What? Davis is a great guy.

JOHNSON OK—shut up—we should probably start studying.

JIMMY You don't think so?

JOHNSON No I do I just think that if we are going to go over everything we learned—I'm just saying that talking about Davis is just not the most, um, productive way to go about—

COOPER What? You don't like Davis?

JOHNSON OK—Enough Davis talk, please.

JIMMY What—did he beat you in Xbox this weekend or something?

JOHNSON YEAH RIGHT!

JIMMY Then what?

JOHNSON I have a perfectly fine relationship with Davis. It's this fool I can't handle.

COOPER Oh—yeah—I'm the core of your issues. Is it dark in that closet?

JOHNSON So should we start with the class notes?

COOPER (*Picking something up off of the ground.*) Johnson, look! I found it!

JIMMY Is that a tooth?

COOPER Yeah it's Jenny fuckin' Abrahamson's tooth.

COOPER *puts the tooth in an empty beer can.*

JIMMY Why do you have Jenny Abrahamson's tooth?

JOHNSON Umm . . .

COOPER Dumb bitch broke it on a beer bottle last night.

COOPER (*writes on a beer can and says as he writes—*) Jenny. Abrahamson's. Tooth.

JIMMY You guys have a party?

COOPER More like a rager.

JOHNSON (*Reading.*) Humans care for their young far longer than any other animal. We're going to have to know that.

COOPER It was our annual one. You know—Tunnel of Love. No cameras. No Facebook. You should have been here. You actually, really should have been here.

JIMMY Who showed up?

COOPER Everyone. I wouldn't even be able to pick anyone out of a line up.

JIMMY Who got laid? Any shockers?

COOPER Hey Johnson—who would you say lucked out the most last night?

JOHNSON (*Not paying attention.*) Me. 'Cause I left.

COOPER No. I mean of who got laid. Besides you-know-who. (*Beat.*)

JOHNSON Hey Jimmy—if you don't have your wits about you for this test, you might resort to cheating, and if anybody finds out about the cheating, then they might lose their fucking temper, ok Cooper? And I don't want any part in that.

JIMMY So I'm guessing Johnson didn't get laid.

COOPER Not by a girl, at least.

JIMMY So who lucked out?

COOPER Johnson, you-know-who!

JIMMY Who, Johnson? Who?

JOHNSON (*Slow and livid. Through his teeth.*) I don't know, Cooper. Who?

COOPER You have no idea who I'm talking about?

JOHNSON Wait—do I? Wait—now I really have no idea if we are talking about the same person.

COOPER Well who are you talking about?

JOHNSON I don't wanna say.

JIMMY Why?

JOHNSON Cooper?

COOPER I think we're talking about the same person. Are you talking about . . .

JOHNSON (*Almost whispered.*) . . . Davis?

JIMMY DAVIS?!

COOPER JOHNSON!

JOHNSON That's why I—Well who were *you* talking about?!

JIMMY Aw man! It's about time! Good for him, man. Who was the lucky girl?

JOHNSON Uh . . . You probably don't know her.

JIMMY Bullshit. I know everyone.

JOHNSON Well I'm going to go order some food. Is Chinese good for everyone?

COOPER Jimmy, you should probably study. I'll leave you fools alone.

JIMMY No no no—you can't tell me that Davis the Good gets laid and then not tell me which bitch got nailed. Was it a freshman? (*Beat.*) Does that mean I'm right? (*Beat.*) Spill the shit man. Who was the girl? (*Beat.*) What's going on here? Why are you guys pussying out on me? (*Beat.*) Why don't you want me to know? (*Beat.*) Oh fuck. (*Beat.*) Oh *fuck*.

COOPER Way to go, Johnson.

JOHNSON Oh fuck you.

COOPER Honestly, Jimmy, I'm glad you heard it from us.

JOHNSON Jimmy, I'm sorry, but for the record, I was not here. I had gone home and was not present at the time. (*Beat.*)

JIMMY I'm gonna kill her.

SCENE 5

An American Flag. A projection screen. Bizarre, tacky lighting. The sounds of a convention. Almost a carnival. This is a meeting for the Future Leaders of America.

GRACE Hello future leaders! It is my great honor to welcome you to the 36th Semi-Annual Future Leaders of America Conference. I am Grace Byrnes, your elected President, and I am going to say a couple of words before we begin our retreat. First of all, you'll have to excuse my hand. In an effort to be well-rounded, I misstepped and am now dealing with the consequences. I won't fully believe in equal rights until I see a man in a business skirt and heels. That said, I want to congratulate everybody here tonight and tomorrow for participating in these events. The people in this room represent a new generation. Growing up we were told, "Don't worry about what others think of you." And boy do they regret teaching us that one because now we are facing a generational vice. Research shows that amongst our peers the central concern for each individual is on the me. The I. The I. The me. Me. I. iPhone. MEphone. My turn. Me first. A line? I don't have to wait. A price? I don't have to pay. A test? I don't have to study. A generation of self-awareness and self concern— where *they* make what *we* want and what we want is more me. Facebook. Twitter. All social media. We are the members of a generation that has been dubbed Generation Me.

But as I stand here, in front of my peers, in front of the best and brightest and the most promising minds, I am forced to find the

good in us. The good in me. The good in you. And at the end of
my search, I have found our redeeming quality. The gem of this
generation, and the upside to our selfishness, is the invincibility
we espouse. Sure, we may consider that the rules do not apply
to us, but for those of us still hungry to succeed in this world, our
redeeming quality is that we look at obstacles in the same way.
How do we do this? The *successful* members of Generation Me,
the iGeneration, have a secret weapon. This weapon is composed
of defiance and denial and greed, and yet is more precious than
gold. The weapon, our weapon, is the desire and tendency to
answer a simple question: What can I do to make this work? In
any situation, what can I do to get what I want? Some people,
after college, will move back home and sit in their parents' base-
ments, blaming the unpredictable economy and the truly bizarre
job market. That's how they will make this world work for them.
But not us. The ones who refuse to take no for an answer. We will
make our way in spite of the fact that the America this generation
has been given is not the America that this generation was told
we would get. Is this the land of opportunity? No. Now we're
dealing with the land of strategy. Obstacles? We must see none.
Dilemmas? They must be all the more fun. We will succeed. We
just have to find a way. And if you don't want to be a victim of
this mess, my advice is to *find any way*. So after the festivities of
tomorrow end, and after we adjourn for another half of a year,
I will be proud to be a representative of not only the Future
Leaders of America, but more importantly of Generation Me. Like
us or not, this is what we've got. Who knew hell and high water
could be exciting! Thank you. And let's have fun tonight!

SCENE 6

The girls' apartment. LEIGH *is cleaning the kitchen. After a few moments,* JIMMY *tries the locked door, and then knocks on it.* LEIGH *crosses to the door and opens it.*

LEIGH Hey. Come in. I'm just cleaning up.

JIMMY *enters and sits on the couch.* LEIGH *continues cleaning. Silence for a few minutes. As* LEIGH *cleans . . .*

LEIGH I'm screwed for midterms.

She continues to clean. JIMMY *sits. Silence.*

LEIGH I called the bank to tell them about my loans, but I completely forgot that today is Sunday so I'm going to call back tomorrow.

Silence.

LEIGH Jimmy? Pooks—are you listening to me?

JIMMY You know last night, on the beach, I was at an empty bar. It was one of the best nights of my life. I was sitting in the sand, looking out at the ocean, and just thinking about how small I was, but how big I felt. And I thought about all the times I had fucked up in the past twenty-one years, and all the things I would take back. And I realized how peaceful I felt. And how I was alone with all of this sand and all of this water to myself. And I didn't feel lonely at all, because I loved you so much. And I didn't feel like I'd fucked up at all because I knew that I was going to love you so much. (*Beat.*) What did you do last night? I want you to be honest.

LEIGH Ok . . .

Silence.

JIMMY Come on, just say it. (*Beat.*) Just fucking say it, Leigh.

LEIGH Where were you just now?

JIMMY At the party. It might not look like it, but for me it's still going on.

LEIGH At Rafter's?

JIMMY At your boyfriend's house, Leigh. At the fucking party of the year.

LEIGH What did they tell you?

JIMMY Don't.

LEIGH Jimmy—you tell me what they told you.

JIMMY They didn't have to say anything. Sadly, I could figure it out all on my own.

LEIGH Don't. That's not fair. You weren't there.

JIMMY Ha—That didn't stop you before.

LEIGH I don't need this. You can show yourself out.

JIMMY You have about this much room to talk right now. And even that might be generous. Come on, Leigh. I want to hear it straight from the whore's mouth.

LEIGH You are a spoiled rotten jackass, you know that Jimmy?

JIMMY I should have left you on the other side of the tracks. I guess you can't teach a poor dog new tricks.

LEIGH You are going to feel like such a fool.

JIMMY Going to? You've already played that trick on me, sweetie. There's not much lower that I can feel.

LEIGH Just hear me out—

JIMMY Like Davis did? "Oh fuck me. Fuck me, Davis! Harder! Fuck me harder! My boyfriend is far away, being loyal, so he'll never hear me screaming your name!"

LEIGH That's not how it was.

JIMMY I have done everything for you! So if you could do me the honor of telling me the details, you can maybe ruin the idea of "trust" for me a little more.

LEIGH Everyone was drunk—

JIMMY And you were drinking?!

LEIGH Everyone was drunk—That's the only way I can—

JIMMY What about you, Leigh?

LEIGH Please. Please, Jimmy. Please. (*Beat.*) He wanted to show me a picture from freshman year, he said. So I went into his room and I sat on his bed. (*Beat.*)

JIMMY Leigh—

LEIGH He handed me his phone and told me to find it in there. He came around to look with me as I flipped through. His face was right next to mine. I turned to look at him and he kissed me. And I pulled away. He was drunk, Jimmy, and then . . .

JIMMY I can't believe this.

LEIGH He took my hand and he . . . placed it. There.

JIMMY Stop.

LEIGH And I tried to get out of there. I tried to get Grace, but before I could go his hands were digging into my shoulders and he just like . . . threw me down, Jimmy. It was really loud in the other room. I tried to stop him but his hand was on my face and I just screamed "NO! STOP!"

JIMMY Wait—what?

LEIGH I kept hoping that someone would hear me but I couldn't breathe in enough air.

JIMMY Davis?

LEIGH I couldn't move.

JIMMY Good Davis?

LEIGH Get off. Get off of his side.

JIMMY I'm not on his side.

LEIGH I could barely breathe. I couldn't scream. So I just tried to count down from 200 'cause I figured it'd be over by then. And then—you know—when he was done, he loosened his hand from around my neck and I whispered "No. Please. Please, Davis. No." But it didn't matter. It had happened. And I looked around the room. And you were out of town. And Grace was out of sight. And I was alone. Being fucked. So fuck you.

JIMMY That's a lot.

LEIGH I fucking hate you, Jimmy.

JIMMY Leigh—

LEIGH No. Don't touch me. You're one of them!

JIMMY I don't know what to think!

LEIGH Thank you. Thank you for that.

JIMMY Well I don't want to believe that's true. I mean you understand that, right?

LEIGH How could I? I'm just a poor whore.

JIMMY Don't.

LEIGH You should journal about this and take it to your Christian therapist.

JIMMY I was clearly flipping out because I was pissed.

LEIGH But now that you know I was raped, you're not so mad anymore?

JIMMY Whoa.

LEIGH Yeah. Whoa. Fucking whoa. I really thought you were going to save me. I thought the life I lived before you, I thought all of that was in the past and that I grew up with nothing just to balance out how lucky I would become when I met you.

JIMMY Look---Leigh—you have to see where I was coming from. We were both lucky to find each other. And to have each other. We were meant for each other.

LEIGH HA!

JIMMY We're gonna have a kid together! (*Beat.*) I mean, right? (*Beat.*) Leigh? (*Beat.*) Leigh. What?

LEIGH I came home and I crawled into Grace's bed. She had fallen asleep in mine. I woke up and the sheets were soaked in blood. I had to hide them so Grace wouldn't see.

LEIGH *pulls* GRACE*'s bloody sheets out of the laundry bag.*

JIMMY Oh my God.

LEIGH It just happened.

JIMMY No.

LEIGH I couldn't stop it. I'm sorry.

JIMMY Leigh no. No.

LEIGH The baby—our baby—

JIMMY Oh my God. No. Leigh. Oh fuck. Oh Jesus. Why didn't you tell me?

LEIGH Because it just happened.

JIMMY Oh Leigh. I love you. I love you, sweetheart.

LEIGH Will you hold me?

JIMMY I love you so much.

LEIGH I know.

Beat as they stay in the hug and he kisses her head.

JIMMY We have to tell my dad.

LEIGH No.

JIMMY We do. He can help. He can take care of Davis.

LEIGH But we can't tell him about the baby.

JIMMY We have to.

LEIGH That'll hurt us, Jimmy. Two irresponsible kids?

JIMMY You have to let me do this.

LEIGH But nothing will change, right?

JIMMY What do you—

LEIGH Promise me that nothing will change.

JIMMY Nothing will—

LEIGH   You'll stay. With me. You'll stay.

JIMMY   Of course I'm going to stay with you.

LEIGH   And the baby. You'll say nothing.

JIMMY   I'll—

LEIGH   Promise me.

JIMMY   Ok. All right. I promise.

LEIGH   Good. Ok, good. Oh Jimmy. (*Beat.*) Now can you help me clean these sheets?

SCENE 7

The boys' house. It is morning.

*DAVIS is asleep on top of his books on the coffee table. COOPER
tip-toes in, sees that DAVIS is sleeping, and goes for his iPad. In the
middle of this, DAVIS's cell phone rings. DAVIS abruptly wakes up
and COOPER tip-toe runs back into his room. DAVIS scrambles to find
his phone.*

DAVIS Hello? This is him. Today? Hold on—let me grab a pen and
paper. Actually I have a midterm at one, but any time after . . .
umm, Ok. Ok. I'll be there at one. May I ask what this is regarding?
Oh ok. Sure.

DAVIS hangs up and sits. He ponders. He needs an answer.

DAVIS COOPER! COOPER, GET OUT HERE!

DAVIS runs and opens COOPER's bedroom door.

DAVIS Wake up. Cooper wake up!

COOPER Huh? What man? Get out I'm sleeping.

DAVIS Cooper, now. Now.

COOPER comes out of his room as though he just woke up.

COOPER Ugh—Can you get the fuck out?

DAVIS What did you guys talk about last night?

COOPER Who?

DAVIS Now, Cooper.

COOPER You mean Johnson and Jimmy?

DAVIS Yes. I mean Johnson and Jimmy. What did you guys talk about?

COOPER Oh you know—we just shot the shit. Johnson read off a few factoids, we talked about some other stuff.

DAVIS You told him, didn't you?

COOPER I'm so tired.

DAVIS Fuck, Cooper!

COOPER I didn't say anything. Johnson is the one who said your name.

DAVIS What the hell kind of friend are you?

COOPER All I said was that Jenny Abrahamson lost a tooth and then he asked if we had a party and then—

DAVIS Does he know enough to actually be mad at me?

COOPER Oh he knows. But he didn't even say anything about you, dude. He was just really mad at Leigh. You know Jimmy, he's a dumbass.

DAVIS This is not good.

COOPER Relax, man. You're not even friends with Jimmy.

DAVIS I just got a call from the dean's secretary. He wants to meet today at one.

COOPER Oh shit.

DAVIS Yeah.

COOPER Well so what? Maybe it's about something completely unrelated.

DAVIS He told me not to go to my midterms.

COOPER That's bad. Yeah that's bad.

DAVIS What the hell am I going to do?

COOPER *gets a text message [Are you up?].*

COOPER Just tell him the truth. You can't get in trouble for having sex with someone. I mean she's over eighteen, right? And even though Jimmy's dad is on the board, that doesn't make this an academic issue. So you're in the clear.

DAVIS Yeah. It's not a crime. It was dick of me, but it's not a crime.

COOPER Right.

DAVIS Yeah.

COOPER But it is weird that he told you not to go to your midterm.

DAVIS Actually the words were "Suspend attending all of your classes."

COOPER Suspend? You're suspended?

DAVIS I guess I am. What the fuck?

COOPER What all did you do to her? Did you fuck her eyes out or something?

COOPER *'s cell phone rings. He answers.*

COOPER What do you want? Christ, Johnson, I don't know. Hold on. Davis, do you see Johnson's three-hole puncher anywhere?

DAVIS *holds it up.*

COOPER Yeah. It's here. Come get it. No—you come get it. I don't know, what the hell does it matter when Davis will be here? Uh-huh. Uh-huh. You're joking. Oh. Yeah. I'll bring it to practice. Bye.

DAVIS What was that?

COOPER Umm—nothing.

DAVIS What did he say?

COOPER Hey—Davis—tell me again what happened on Saturday night. With Leigh.

DAVIS Why?

COOPER You know, practice. It'll be good to go over it.

DAVIS Uh—ok. We went into my bedroom . . . I don't want to do this right now.

COOPER It'd be good for you.

DAVIS The details don't matter.

COOPER *gets a text message. Then another. Then another. He silences his phone.*

DAVIS What's going on?

COOPER Was she into it? (*Beat.*)

DAVIS What?

COOPER Was she—

DAVIS Cooper. Stop.

COOPER Was she ok with it, I mean? (*Beat.*) Davis—I won't tell. (*Beat.*)

DAVIS *is frozen.*

DAVIS What? No I—I didn't do that, Cooper.

COOPER Ok.

DAVIS I don't think I'd have it in me even if I wanted to.

COOPER Then tell me what happened.

DAVIS You know what happened—your ear was pressed against the door you said.

COOPER Davis—I was pretty drunk and everyone was being loud. Just tell me what happened—and that way I can believe you. If you don't tell me then I only know one side of the story.

DAVIS What did Johnson just say to you?

COOPER Davis—

DAVIS What did she say to him?

DAVIS *goes after* COOPER*'s phone.* COOPER *shields it from* DAVIS.

COOPER Come on. Come on. Come on, man.

DAVIS Don't you—you have to be—

COOPER You should shower before your meeting.

DAVIS Are you FUCKING KIDDING ME?!

COOPER Come on.

DAVIS Are you KIDDING ME?!

COOPER I mean she's lying, right?

DAVIS I'll fucking punch her out.

COOPER Don't say that.

DAVIS No fuck you. I'm not that person. You know I'm not that person.

COOPER It doesn't matter if I do or not. I'm your friend no matter what.

DAVIS I need you to believe me.

COOPER Then tell me what happened.

DAVIS Holy shit!

COOPER Just tell me what happened!

DAVIS I DON'T KNOW! (*Beat.*) I don't remember, ok? Fuck!

COOPER What are you talking about?

DAVIS I don't even remember having sex with her. I just said that stuff so you guys would leave me alone about it.

COOPER Whoa. Davis—it will all work out.

DAVIS How? I don't have a defense. OH MY GOD!

COOPER Just think.

DAVIS MOTHER FUCKER! GOD DAMN IT!

COOPER Davis—just bring it down, buddy.

COOPER *tries to put his hand on* DAVIS*'s back to comfort him.*

DAVIS FUCK!

DAVIS *takes* COOPER *by the collar and shoves him against the wall, pinning him.*

COOPER Davis! Davis!

A moment and then, realizing the rage he is capable of, DAVIS *backs away.*

DAVIS Oh shit. Cooper.

DAVIS *looks at his hands, realizing what he is capable of.*

Oh fuck.

ACT II

SCENE 1

Future Leaders of America Conference.

GRACE What are you about? In life. In your goals.

GRACE *searches her pockets one last time.*

I had a speech written for this and I just . . . just keep your belongings close, everyone. I know I yelled this countless times at the mixer but it's a brown, leather, Louis Vuitton bag and it has everything in it. My glasses, my phone, my speech. So if you find anything that doesn't belong to you, please return it to . . . you know, me. 'Cause—well—because, you know— it's mine.

Ok. I know it. I have my original notes somewhere I think but I'll just—I'm going to talk to you all directly. Just sort of wing it. We're all friends here, right?

Ok.

Future leaders: we have all proven ourselves in some way or another to get here today. Everybody here strives for success. For greatness. Some of us for theft, but most of us for greatness. But as we conclude our conference, I want each of you to put some thought into this question: What are you about? What is the *one thing* that you want?

We all want to be great, right? Well while a great part of the formula for success is the ability to roll with the punches and say yes to what you are given, a great part of the formula for excellence is knowing when to say no. When to examine an opportunity, no matter how enticing it may be, and have the ability to weigh it next to *what you are about.*

A balloon is not a Crockpot. Who wouldn't want to slow cook a delicious dinner with the push of a button? It doesn't get much better than that. But a balloon cannot be a balloon and a Crockpot.

Ok—I know I have my original notes around here somewhere. It just gets a little complicated and I just want to make sure that you all—

She takes a cue from someone offstage.

I know I know—we're running out of time. My mother always told me that I was going to have to deal with her bad karma. She stole Meredith Powers's science fair project in the early 70s and Meredith failed and my mother—anyway—it's happening. Ok—what I was saying. A balloon is not a Crockpot. It can't cook a meal.

Back on track.

And even if it could, even if a balloon could say yes to this ridiculous idea, making food in itself, it would never fly quite so high if it was also cooking a turkey dinner at the same time.

It's not registering but she moves on anyway.

And what about that Crockpot? Say it got balloon envy and floated away. Even if it was the best Crockpot ever made, what good is it now? You have to believe me that this was a very great speech. But I hope you get the point. You have to be a balloon or be a Crockpot. You have to do what you can do best. You owe that to yourself. Your first priority is you, always. That's what we've been taught by those who came before us, and we have learned from the best. (*Beat.*)

Ok. That's it. The conference has ended. The time has come to return from whence you came. I have been a part of this organization since I was eleven years old, and it was an honor to be your president this year. I will be speaking at next year's conference in an effort to pass on whatever I can to the generation after us. We have got the world at our fingertips my fellow balloons. Or Crockpots. Or staplers or wallpaper or tambourines. Anyway. You are young. You are promising. You are you. And we . . . we are the Future Leaders of America. *(Beat.)*

She walks off totally disgraced.

SCENE 2

The girls' apartment. LEIGH *stands, holding her cell phone. It's flipped open. Immediately—*

VOICEMAIL LADY (*From the phone.*) You have seven new messages. First message:

HALEY (*Through the phone.*) Hey hon it's Haley. After we talked last night—

LEIGH *hits delete.*

VOICEMAIL LADY Deleted. Next Message.

HALEY Sorry—I got cut . . .

Delete.

VOICEMAIL LADY Deleted. Next Message.

HALEY I hope you're ok. I . . .

Delete.

VOICEMAIL LADY Deleted. Next Message.

HALEY Leigh I'm worried that . . .

Delete.

VOICEMAIL LADY Deleted. Next Message.

HALEY Is this . . .

VOICEMAIL LADY Deleted. Next Message.

HALEY You had better . . . !

VOICEMAIL LADY Deleted. Next Message.

HALEY WHY WO . . . ?!?!

VOICEMAIL LADY Deleted. No new messages.

HALEY (*From offstage, approaching, yelling.*) I'm here! LEIGH! LEIGH
OPEN YOUR DOOR!

There is a knock at the door.

LEIGH Shit.

She opens the door.

HALEY *is holding a bottle of wine and a balloon.*

HALEY This is for you. Well come on. Put your arms around me and
let's do what normal girls do when they haven't seen each other
in a while.

LEIGH I'm not going to let you weasel your way into this.

HALEY Into what?

LEIGH You need to leave.

HALEY No. Not gonna happen. I packed up for this and came all
the way up here! I cannot believe Jimmy had to call me and tell
me to check in on you. Were you really not going to tell me this
was going on?

LEIGH You are not involved in this, do you understand me?

HALEY Is that why it took you two hours to pick up one of my calls
last night?

LEIGH Yes!

HALEY We're movin' on up, Sis! And I'll be here to help you deal with
your convenient tragedy.

LEIGH Haley—listen—I would rather you not stay.

HALEY Well I'd rather be able to afford a Heineken but sometimes bitch just gotta drink Miller Light. What kind of sister would I be if I just let you deal with this whole thing on your own?

LEIGH One who was respectful of my wishes?

HALEY Yeah. That'll be the day. How's college life? Generations of our ancestors are dying to know. I like what you've done with the place. Very "dressing for the job you want" of you.

LEIGH The lease is up in two months. Where are you living?

HALEY With Rico at the Super 8 in Waterbury. You wouldn't believe it. More trouble with the lawsuit. Get this— Apparently . . . you can't sue a child.

LEIGH Why is he trying to sue a child?

HALEY But he's promised me a Pomeranian.

LEIGH Well I hope it works out.

HALEY Me too. Though we've been having trouble communicating lately. It might just be the language barrier, but I have this fear that if his English was better we'd find out that we have nothing in common. And that scares me, Leigh. It really does. But, you know, as long as I get my Pomeranian. So . . . come on . . . What's new with you?

LEIGH Well I mean the past couple of days have been kind of rough.

HALEY No no. Just 'cause you got raped doesn't mean that's all that's happening in the world. I want to know what's going on with *you*.

LEIGH This is so—

HALEY Have you seen any new movies?

LEIGH You have to be nicer to me.

HALEY Oh, Leigh. You know that somewhere, in the back of your mind, tucked under all of your "despair" this ended up being a good thing.

LEIGH This situation is super fragile, ok? Why did you think that it was alright to come up here?

HALEY Well I'm going to protect you first and foremost. But I'm also here to watch the girl who always lands on her feet.

LEIGH I'm just doing what I have to do.

HALEY Alright—so let's talk. This guy. The defendant. Is he hot?

LEIGH HALEY!

HALEY What is he telling people? Let's go over there and get a confession out of him. I'm wearing a new bra and my cell phone records things even through my bag.

LEIGH We're not going anywhere.

HALEY We need to lock this up and shut this down, Leigh. If Jimmy leaves you, I'll have no way to make Rico feel bad about himself. And then how else am I supposed to *get things*?

LEIGH I have to go get my laundry before Grace gets back.

HALEY Fine. Fine. We'll talk about something else. You're also being very secretive about what movies you've seen so I don't know what there is left to talk about.

LEIGH Look—I'm not required to let you stay here.

HALEY Better to keep me close, girlie. If I'm on the loose, you just don't know *what* I'll do.

LEIGH Haley?

HALEY I'm either for you or against you. What'll it be? (*Beat.*)

LEIGH Where are you going to sleep?

HALEY In your bed.

LEIGH No.

HALEY Can't you sleep at Jimmy's? He's not leaving you, right?

LEIGH No.

HALEY I mean post-"miscarriage" he's still loving you, right?

LEIGH Lucky enough, yes.

HALEY Good. The last thing I need is your poor ass all alone in the big bad world. You got any chips?

LEIGH Chips?

HALEY Chips. Salty. Tostitos. Doritos. Chips. You got chips?

LEIGH You can check the pantry.

HALEY Pantry. Listen to you. "Pantry." From food bucket to pantry. Wouldn't Dad be proud.

LEIGH Who?

HALEY You know. Think back. Dad. Dad. The man with the belt and the beer.

LEIGH Nope. Must have blocked him out.

HALEY I remember him whenever I want to wear a backless shirt.

HALEY *laughs, trying to connect with* LEIGH *on that. No luck.*

Come on. He was always screwing that woman who never fed us.
You remember. Asking Mom for lunch?

LEIGH It's not something real people eat.

HALEY It only happened on TV.

LEIGH How the hell did she come up with that?

HALEY How the hell did we believe that bitch for so long?

LEIGH I don't know. But thank God for Daniel Decker.

HALEY What? Why?

LEIGH I would always make sure that I was playing with him around
noon so that his mom would invite me in for some food.

HALEY And you didn't tell me?

LEIGH You always tried to kiss Daniel Decker and then he'd run
away.

HALEY I was starving. For years. I used to go to bed early so
I wouldn't be awake to feel the hungry.

LEIGH Daniel's mom would make like turkey and cheese
sandwiches. Not steak. Chill out.

HALEY You stupid cunt.

LEIGH Haley!

HALEY It will always be the same, won't it? Everything works out
for you. You play tag with Daniel Decker and you get a good meal
on the table. You lie to Jimmy about being pregnant so the fool
will stay with you and then you are lucky enough to get raped.
Everything falls right into your lap.

LEIGH I wasn't lucky Haley. That boy rejected me for years and the one time I say "no" he thinks "yes."

HALEY Well if you didn't have something to blame the miscarriage on, you would have to produce a baby in nine months and we get CNN at the Super 8 and I know that when people steal babies from hospitals, it never works out.

LEIGH Oh come on, I would never steal a baby.

HALEY I wouldn't put it past you.

LEIGH God—am I a monster? Is that what everyone thinks?

HALEY Maybe. But that doesn't mean bad shit can't happen to you too. Did you do what we used to do?

LEIGH What?

HALEY Did you count down from 200?

LEIGH *nods.*

Ok. Anyway, I think I want to start taking classes.

LEIGH Really?

HALEY Yeah! Isn't this exciting?

LEIGH What kind of classes?

HALEY Just classes. That's as far as I've gotten.

LEIGH Hey—that's step one.

HALEY And once this is all said and done, I'll have the money to afford them.

LEIGH Don't talk like that.

HALEY Oh honey, I got no problem being a dog as long as someone throws me a bone. I've also decided that I am going to only wear shirts with low low necklines. It's time for me to start taking control of my life.

LEIGH Alright. You sit here. Don't move. Don't touch anything. Don't talk to anyone. I'm going to get my laundry. You've got your chips right? You're good with the chips? Just sit and stay. Do you understand me?

HALEY Woof woof. Tail wag. Ear flop. Poop in your bed.

HALEY *stares at* LEIGH.

LEIGH *exits.*

HALEY *looks around the apartment. She picks up a pillow and looks at the tag on it.*

HALEY Crate and Barrel?

After a beat, she puts the pillow down on the couch, unbuckles her pants and pulls them down just enough so that her butt is out. She rubs her butt on the pillow.

GRACE *enters through the front door.*

GRACE (*As she enters.*) Hello?!

HALEY *frantically pulls up her pants.*

HALEY I wasn't even doing anything!

GRACE Oh! I'm sorry. Umm . . . Can I help you with something? Where's Leigh?

HALEY She had to go get her laundry.

GRACE I'm Grace.

HALEY I figured. I've heard so much about you. I'm Haley. Her sister.

GRACE   Oh my God! I thought you'd never come visit!

HALEY   Leigh told me that you didn't like house guests.

GRACE   What? That's not true. (*Beat.*) Well this is great. When did you get in?

HALEY   Not long ago. I like your bandage.

GRACE   That's weird but thank you. (*Beat.*) So . . . What's been going on?

SCENE 3

Boys' house.

JOHNSON *is playing Xbox. A beat and then* DAVIS *enters.* JOHNSON *does not move his attention.* DAVIS *sits on the couch—defeated.*

DAVIS Stupid.

JOHNSON What?

DAVIS Everything.

JOHNSON *looks at* DAVIS.

JOHNSON DAVIS!

DAVIS Yeah? What?

JOHNSON I thought you were going to be gone all afternoon. That's what Cooper said.

DAVIS Well I'm back. Stop flipping out. Play your games.

JOHNSON No. I should probably go.

DAVIS No—Johnson—just hang out. I'm not having the best day.

JOHNSON (*Hesitantly.*) Alright.

DAVIS Life is crazy, Johnson.

JOHNSON Yeah. (*Beat.*) So we good? Can I go?

DAVIS Johnson—

JOHNSON Sorry, Davis. It's just midterms and everything all happening. I'd love to hang out with you it's just, you know, a bad time.

DAVIS Yeah—well—I mean go if you have to but I'm kind of up a creek right now.

JOHNSON Look—don't do that.

DAVIS Do what?

JOHNSON Don't make me feel bad.

DAVIS How am I trying to make you—

JOHNSON Because I don't want to be around you.

DAVIS I started to get that feeling.

JOHNSON It's nothing personal.

DAVIS I'm taking it that way.

JOHNSON Oh bring it on. Bring on the guilt.

DAVIS I've barely said two words.

JOHNSON God you are so selfish.

DAVIS What did I do now?

JOHNSON Look—we get along—we've been buddies.

DAVIS Been?

JOHNSON I just can't afford to be with you right now.

DAVIS Jesus, Johnson, we're not dating. You were playing video games and I was sitting on the couch.

JOHNSON Come on. Don't play dumb. And now Natalie is saying all of these things.

DAVIS No. No. What is she saying?!

JOHNSON I'm not getting involved, Davis! You'd do the same thing if you were me.

DAVIS I'd ditch my friend because he's upset?

JOHNSON Davis—

DAVIS What? Hear that someone was accusing him of something awful and then do my best to stay away from him?

JOHNSON Come on.

DAVIS No. Tell me. Tell me what I would do, Johnson. Buddy.

JOHNSON Look this whole thing is a pretty big deal, alright? A big fuckin' deal. I go to bed early every night. I can count on one and a half hands the number of times I've been drunk. I am a cautious motherfucker. I haven't been able to breathe for all twenty-one years of my life because I am trying, desperately, to become the man that I want to be. And I'm sorry, but there are just too many ways to fuck that up. And I won't allow it.

DAVIS So what, you don't believe me?

JOHNSON Of course I believe you, Davis. I know you. I know you wouldn't do that.

DAVIS Then what's your deal?

JOHNSON Not everybody knows you. Not the dean. Not my parents. Not the press.

DAVIS So what?

JOHNSON And don't tell me I'm not a good friend, because I am. I sit in class and watch you doodle while I scramble to find a blank page in my notebook. And it's like clockwork. I schedule time before a test to help you before you even ask. And I've never once bitched. I come to your house for parties when you know full well that I hate parties. I hate them. Not exaggerating. But I come because I'm a good friend. And when Natalie dumped you, I was the only one who didn't curse her out right away because I knew you still loved her and didn't want to see her get hurt, regardless of the shit she put you through. Why? Because I am a good friend, Davis. You should know that. So, I'm sorry if on the eve of my graduation from college I don't want to be thrown into the midst of a scandal, and knowing your parents and Leigh's background quite possibly a national scandal, regardless of who's right or wrong.

DAVIS Wow, man. Well good for you.

JOHNSON Be a good friend, Davis. Don't bring me down with you.

DAVIS Alright.

JOHNSON I'm sorry.

DAVIS Yeah. You are.

JOHNSON See you in ten years.

JOHNSON *exits.* DAVIS *picks up the phone and hesitates as he fights back tears. He dials. A few beats.*

DAVIS Hey, Mom. It's me. Sorry I haven't returned your phone calls. Umm. I have kind of some bad news. I don't really know what to tell you. It's pretty bad. Just call me back when you get this, ok? I love you. Mom, I love you.

DAVIS *hangs up the phone.*

DAVIS (*To the phone.*) Sorry.

DAVIS *is broken. A few beats and then* COOPER *enters.*

COOPER Davis? Holy shit. Davis? Oh—what happened? Hey man— what happened?

DAVIS It's over.

COOPER What is?

DAVIS My life! Done. Bury me now.

DAVIS *is throwing away all of this school items.*

COOPER No it's not, Davis. Whatever's going on, we can beat it, man. Did you meet with the dean?

DAVIS Yeah. I didn't say anything. He just talked. I have to go to a special hearing tomorrow to plead either way so they can figure out what to do with me.

COOPER What do you mean?

DAVIS Well if I say not guilty then they are going to gather all of the evidence and have a trial but if I say guilty then they are going to have to figure out how to punish me which looks like I might get expelled.

COOPER Oh God. That sucks, man.

DAVIS And then there's the legal matter. Like if she presses charges then I am done, you know? Game over. I lose.

COOPER You just gotta take this one step at a time man.

DAVIS And then Johnson—

COOPER Johnson's a douchebag, man. We hate Johnson.

DAVIS But he's doing exactly what I want to do. He's running.

COOPER Don't worry. We'll call a lawyer. We'll fight this.

DAVIS No.

COOPER Yes we will.

DAVIS No—I'm pleading no contest.

COOPER What? Why? That's stupid, Davis. You're thinking stupid.

DAVIS Fuck you, Cooper. I don't have a chance in hell. I don't have a case. I fucked up. If this goes to trial it is just going to draw more attention to the whole thing and I can't do that. I can't put my family through that. Or the team. And then they're just going to find me guilty anyway because they are going to ask me what actually happened and I'm just going to like stand there blubbering something because I can't actually answer the question.

COOPER You're rich. You're white. You shouldn't have a problem.

DAVIS That works against me, Cooper. Don't you get that?

COOPER You really don't remember anything?

DAVIS I really, really don't. (*Beat.*)

COOPER Then you need to try to fix this, man. (*Beat.*)

DAVIS I really thought I was starting to get control over things.

DAVIS *goes to exit.*

COOPER Hey man—where are you going?

DAVIS I don't know. Don't wait up.

SCENE 4

A laundromat. LEIGH *is finishing folding her laundry.* GRACE *enters, observing.*

LEIGH Surprise—I thought you'd like some fresh linens.

GRACE Wow. Thank you.

LEIGH Yep. And I bleached them. Look at that. Completely white.

GRACE That's amazing. (*Beat.*) So. Anything . . . going on?

LEIGH Nope. (*Beat.*)

GRACE So who knows?

LEIGH Who— . . . ?

GRACE Leigh, come on. It's me.

LEIGH Ok.

GRACE I've got you. It's not too late to fix this. I know you told Jimmy but has it gotten back to Davis yet? (*Beat.*) Come on. It's fine. Just tell me what you're saying and we can come up with a plan.

LEIGH Thank you for your concern, Grace, but you're making me a little uncomfortable with the way you're—I just don't think it's any of your business right now.

GRACE Leigh, baby, the words you're using—there are incredible ramifications for this. I know you know that.

LEIGH I do know that. Thank you.

GRACE So let's do what's right here, ok?

LEIGH Wow.

GRACE Well you can't expect me to stand with you on this.

LEIGH Ok. Got it.

GRACE Don't do that to me.

LEIGH I'm not really worried about you right now.

GRACE You're playing with fire.

LEIGH Is that what I'm doing?

GRACE You're making a mess.

LEIGH I couldn't walk.

GRACE When?

LEIGH We got home, and I couldn't walk.

GRACE You were drunk.

LEIGH Ok.

GRACE Aww, Leigh, don't do this. If you want to sleep around, that's your deal. I praise you for the courage. You want to start throwing around accusations though and I will raise my hand with questions.

LEIGH Look, I don't need you to get all pre-law student on me.

GRACE Well Leigh how am I supposed to react? Your sister is in the apartment blabbing on about rape. So tell me what is going on.

LEIGH What do you want to know?

GRACE What happened at the party?!

LEIGH You tell me. It sounds like you have a pretty good idea.

GRACE I have an inkling, yes!

LEIGH You think I made it up.

GRACE You're pretending that you didn't?

LEIGH You know what? I think we're done.

GRACE You can't just ignore this, Leigh! You can't just say it's done!

LEIGH Well you and me, Grace? We're absolutely done.

GRACE Oh *you're* going to throw *me* out?

LEIGH I would love for you to be my friend, but it seems you are unable to give me that.

GRACE That's not how it looks to me.

LEIGH Really? And who the fuck are you?

GRACE I'll tell you who I'm not. An enabler.

LEIGH So you came down here to help me with my lie? Is that it?

GRACE You just don't even think about what position you're putting me in, do you?

LEIGH Don't make this about you, Grace! Stop trying to be an example! Just be Grace! Let me get through this. Just hold my hand and let me get through this.

Beat. LEIGH *extends her hand.* GRACE *just stares at her.*

LEIGH (*Realizing, hurt.*) You really don't believe me. (*Beat.*) There's not even a moment of doubt? You're that sure?

GRACE I was there, Leigh.

LEIGH Not the whole time.

GRACE I was listening!

LEIGH Not the whole time!

GRACE Why are you doing this?!

LEIGH I'm not *doing* anything!

GRACE This is so fucked!

LEIGH This is right!

GRACE BUT IS IT TRUE?! (*Beat.*)

LEIGH What's the point?

GRACE I thought we were more than this.

LEIGH We're not. (*Beat.*) So what do you want from me, Grace?

GRACE I just want you to spread them wider next time. Maybe that way the whole team can fit in. (*Beat.*)

LEIGH No. You want me to confide in you and cry in your arms and then maybe I'll realize that the real person I love has been right here all along. Like you've dreamt. And you'll think "I'm glad I paid her rent and took care of her. It finally paid off." You want me to tell you it's a lie so that you can help me out of it. And you want me to open my legs wider so that you can fit in. (*Beat.*)

GRACE Well now we know where we stand.

GRACE *goes to exit, but first—*

You know, if you're telling the truth about all of this—I hope it hurt.

GRACE *exits.*

Beat.

LEIGH It did.

SCENE 5

Back at the boys' place. A knock on the door. COOPER *opens the door and* HALEY *is standing there in sunglasses and pigtails and dressed to show her cleavage. She's holding her purse and she's a bit flustered.*

HALEY Did you have a party here on Saturday night?

COOPER Why?

HALEY Did you?

COOPER Yeah.

HALEY Oh thank God. I couldn't remember where it was.

COOPER Do I know you?

HALEY Is this your place?

COOPER Yeah. Is there something you need?

HALEY Name's Wanda. I was here at that awesome party on Saturday night. I left my pendant here. Would you be kind enough to help me find it?

COOPER Oh sure. Sorry. Let me put on a shirt.

HALEY No no, honey, please. The house comes with a great view.

COOPER What's it look like?

HALEY Athletic and protective.

COOPER No, your pendant.

HALEY It's silver. The chain is. The pendant is blue. And red.

COOPER Blue and red on a silver chain? Do you remember where you were hanging out?

HALEY Just like—here. My God what a party, huh?

COOPER Yeah. Sorry if I don't remember you. It was just so crowded.

HALEY I figured you wouldn't. You were busy with that girl all night.

COOPER Which girl?

HALEY You know. About this tall. Pretty. Could be my sister.

COOPER I wasn't really busy with anyone.

HALEY You live here, don't you? (*Beat.*)

COOPER *stops and looks at* HALEY. *He's suddenly uneasy about her being there.*

COOPER Hey—listen—why don't you give me your number and I'll text you if it turns up.

HALEY Oh—do you have somewhere you have to be?

COOPER I have to—

HALEY I'd like to keep looking.

COOPER I get that, but now's not a good time.

HALEY You mean for the police to come to your house?

COOPER What?

HALEY I'd hate to have to call the police and tell them about my stolen pendant.

COOPER No one stole your pendant.

HALEY Well there's only one way to be sure of that, isn't there?

Beat, as they stare at each other. COOPER *starts to look again.*

COOPER I fucking hate today.

HALEY *strategically places her purse, positioning it so that one side is deliberately facing* COOPER.

HALEY So the party—

COOPER (*Looking for the necklace.*) Fucking stupid party.

HALEY You didn't have fun? A good-looking guy like you? In a great house like this? Do you live here all alone?

COOPER Do you THINK I live here all alone?

HALEY Was I somehow offensive just now?

COOPER Can you wait outside, please?

HALEY No! Ooh—you hate that word don't you?

COOPER What?

HALEY No.

COOPER I promise you that I'll look for your pendant but my roommate might come home soon—

HALEY Roommate?

COOPER Yeah. (*Beat.*)

HALEY He was the one who was busy with that girl all night?

COOPER I don't know what you're talking about. (*Beat.*)

HALEY Ugh. You know what? Just forget it.

She grabs her purse.

You people suck. First, that poor girl leaves this house devastated and now my fucking pendant is missing. You all are gonna get what's coming to you.

HALEY *starts to exit.*

COOPER Devastated?

HALEY What?

COOPER That girl—there was a girl who was . . . devastated? (*Beat.*)

HALEY Mmhm. Yeah.

COOPER Which girl?

HALEY I was standing outside towards the end of the party there was a girl—that girl—and she was crying.

COOPER She was?

HALEY Yeah. And limpin'. I almost got her an ambulance but she was so torn up she couldn't even respond to me.

COOPER Seriously?

HALEY Yeah. Do you know what happened to her?

COOPER What was your name again?

HALEY Wanda. And yours?

COOPER Cooper.

HALEY But the poor girl—short little thing. Her skirt was torn. And I think her leg was bleeding. She musta fell.

COOPER Her skirt was torn?

HALEY Yeah. Bitch musta fell down. Busted a cap. No, that's not right. That's when someone gets shot.

COOPER Do you know the girl's name?

HALEY Lisa? I don't know—her tall, pretty friend had to take her home. What a shame. Everyone else had so much fun at the party.

COOPER And you're sure about this?

HALEY Oh honey—I'm damn sure. When someone looks like they've been hit by a car, you remember.

COOPER Did anyone else see her?

HALEY Tons of people.

Beat, as HALEY *looks at a crystal clock in the room.*

Many witnesses. Ummm . . . is—Christ, is this Waterford?

COOPER What?

HALEY This clock. You have a Waterford clock just sitting in your living room?

COOPER Oh—yeah I guess—our parents kind of put this place together. Could you hear anything while you were outside? I mean before the girl came out?

HALEY Sure. Screaming or something, I'm sure. My Lord. I could probably trade in your silverware for a townhouse.

COOPER Awww no. You could probably just cut through an aluminum can or something.

HALEY Ohhh! That's funny! You're cute and funny! What are you doing later?

COOPER I'll probably be looking for your pendant.

HALEY You want to take me out for a drink?

COOPER Oh my God.

HALEY I put out.

COOPER Here it is.

HALEY What?

COOPER Your pendant.

COOPER *presents* HALLEY *with a pendant from the couch.*

HALEY You are shitting me. HA! Look at that. A blue and red pendant. What are the odds?

COOPER It was in the couch.

HALEY I'm amazing. Well thank you. This is actually really pretty. This is made of real silver! There's a diamond in this!

COOPER I think you should get going now.

HALEY You people don't even know what you have.

COOPER Ok. Listen—I really can't grab that drink.

HALEY Fuck your drink, Cooper. I just got a diamond.

HALEY *exits.* COOPER *thinks for a second, and then picks up his cell phone.*

SCENE 6

The girls' apartment. A beat and then HALEY *comes running into the apartment. In a matter of seconds she is back in her original clothes. She messes up the magazines, knocking most of them onto the floor, and starts reading one while eating her chips.* JIMMY *and* LEIGH *enter.*

LEIGH We're home, Haley! Sorry I was gone so long.

HALEY I was going to send a search party. I've read all of these magazines.

LEIGH Why?

HALEY I got bored. I been sittin' here this whole time.

JIMMY Hi, Haley!

HALEY Hi, Jimmy baby! Long time no see! I missed you.

JIMMY I missed you too. How's Rico?

HALEY He's great. Great. Just got a promotion at Jamba Juice. He's the one you have to ask for the bathroom key now. Real proud. Real proud. Do you have any single friends?

JIMMY Good.

HALEY Maybe family friends?

JIMMY Good. I'm happy for you guys. Haley—you're coming to stay at my place tonight.

HALEY Oh now. He's just kidding, Leigh. I'd never sleep with Jimmy as long as you guys are still together.

LEIGH Oh God, Haley—you're going to sleep at Jimmy's house tonight. I just need some alone time. I have to like check in with myself.

HALEY Ugh. You bitch. Well hold on. Let me use the little girls' room. I'm a gypsy. A freakin' gypsy.

HALEY *exits into the bathroom.*

LEIGH Thanks for taking her tonight.

JIMMY Hey—if that's what you really think you need. (*Beat.*) With everything that's going on with Davis, I almost forget that we also need to allow ourselves time to mourn.

LEIGH How are you doing with that?

JIMMY I love you.

LEIGH I know.

JIMMY'*s phone rings.*

JIMMY Hey—I'm getting a call. Tell Haley to come out to the truck when she's done.

LEIGH Ok.

JIMMY Sleep tight tonight, ok?

LEIGH I will. You too. I'll meet you at the hearing.

JIMMY Ok. Bye.

JIMMY *is in love. He exits.*

LEIGH Haley, hurry up! Jimmy's waiting and it's starting to rain.

HALEY *enters from the bathroom.*

HALEY Ok. Ok. I can't sleep here. I can't pee here.

LEIGH But you've made it your job to make a mess here.

HALEY These fucking magazines. I used to look at these things and think "Fuck you, you rich people with your stupid problems." But then I was like—"No. You know what? I want that. And that's ok." And now, after watching you for all these years, I learned the secret. What it takes to go after what you want. And whenever I see a magazine cover that shows some beautiful person on the cover and says "how they did it," I just laugh. 'Cause I don't need to read it anymore.

JIMMY*'s horn honks*

LEIGH Jimmy's waiting in his truck.

HALEY Ok. Call if you need anything.

LEIGH Hey—Haley? Thank you for believing me.

HALEY *hugs* LEIGH. *After a beat,* LEIGH, *for the first time in a long time, hugs her back.*

HALEY I admire you.

HALEY *exits. As* HALEY *exits,* LEIGH *notices a note taped to her front door. She opens the door again, and pulls the note off of the door before closing it. She reads it aloud.*

LEIGH Grace does not live here anymore. She lost her cell phone, so if you need her, send her a message on Facebook. She will check it every hour. If you're not here for Grace, do yourself a favor and turn around. She's not worth it.

A knock at the door. The door, which was slightly open already, opens wider with the knock.

LEIGH You guys! Did you not see this—

LEIGH *turns to the door.* DAVIS *is revealed to be standing there there, drenched. A beat.*

LEIGH (*Shouting to the other room.*) I'll be right there, Jimmy!

DAVIS I saw him leave. I won't touch you, I swear. (*Beat.*)

LEIGH I'm surprisingly calm right now.

DAVIS Can I come in?

LEIGH Why?

DAVIS Because it's raining.

LEIGH And . . .

DAVIS I'd like to talk to you.

LEIGH Forget it.

DAVIS No. Not talk. I didn't mean talk. I want you to talk to me.

LEIGH What so you can get off to my voice?

DAVIS Please. (*Beat.*) It's just me. It's just Davis. (*Beat.*) Davis. (*Beat.*)

LEIGH When I say leave, you leave.

DAVIS I promise.

LEIGH How can I be sure that you're not going to kill me or something? (*Beat.*) Come in.

DAVIS Thanks.

LEIGH Do you need a towel or something?

DAVIS *nods. She hands him a towel.*

DAVIS Thank you.

LEIGH What am I supposed to say? You're welcome?

DAVIS No I know.

LEIGH You couldn't wait until tomorrow to see me?

DAVIS Look—

LEIGH Ok.

DAVIS I'm sorry.

LEIGH For . . .

DAVIS Everything.

LEIGH Specifically.

DAVIS It's hard to say it.

LEIGH Well it's harder to feel it.

DAVIS You're right.

LEIGH Aww. Thank you.

DAVIS How do I make this right, Leigh?

Beat. LEIGH *shakes her head, looking at the floor.*

DAVIS I'm sorry for Saturday night.

LEIGH Yes.

DAVIS And for how I treated you.

LEIGH Which was how? I've come up with my own vocabulary for the occasion but I'd be interested to hear which words you use.

DAVIS Unimaginable.

Beat.

DAVIS Leigh—I don't remember the evening.

LEIGH I was that forgettable?

DAVIS I was drunk.

LEIGH Not an excuse.

DAVIS You're right. That's not an excuse for my actions. But it does explain why I can't wrap my head around it.

LEIGH So what are you apologizing for? What do you want from me?

DAVIS Can you tell me what happened?

LEIGH If that will make you feel worse.

DAVIS Please?

LEIGH Well what's the last thing you remember?

DAVIS Nothing to do with you.

LEIGH Do you remember seeing each other across the crowd?

DAVIS No.

LEIGH Do you remember asking me to come into your room?

DAVIS No.

LEIGH Do you remember locking the door?

DAVIS No.

LEIGH Do you remember kissing my neck?

DAVIS No.

LEIGH Do you remember me kissing yours? (*Beat.*)

DAVIS No. (*Beat.*)

DAVIS *begins to approach* LEIGH.

LEIGH Do you . . . remember my thighs?

DAVIS No.

LEIGH My nose on your cheek?

DAVIS No.

LEIGH My breath in your mouth?

Beat. DAVIS *is now face to face with* LEIGH. *He leans in.* LEIGH *leans back. After a moment,* DAVIS *leans in further and puts his lips on* LEIGH*'s. He kisses her and after a long moment, she kisses back. They begin to kiss passionately, as* DAVIS *leads her off.*

SCENE 7

The boys' house. A knock. COOPER *opens the door and there stands* JIMMY.

COOPER Hey.

JIMMY If he's here I'll kill him.

COOPER He's not here.

JIMMY I swear, Cooper.

COOPER He's not here. Relax. Chill out. Hold your horses. We're just man to man right now.

JIMMY So what did you want? Why did you call?

COOPER I just need to say a few things to you.

JIMMY Go.

COOPER Jimmy—

JIMMY Go.

Beat.

COOPER Jimmy—you're my friend. We're both sort of in unfortunate positions here.

No response from JIMMY.

I mean Davis is my friend. He's like my brother, you know that.

Nothing.

Ok. And generally, I stand behind him in everything he does and

everything he says. Earlier he told me that the weather was supposed to be nice today. iPhone said rain, he told me nice. There's
a monsoon outside and I'm wearing shorts. Am I making my point?

No response from JIMMY.

I'm thinking I am. Anyway, at the party on Saturday I had my ear
pressed up against the door. Now I was drunk so I don't remember the whole thing. And the next morning I get curious. I want to
know what happened. Whatever Davis says happened, happened.
But he doesn't say anything. There's nothing for me to believe because he doesn't say anything. And that scares me. He's pleading
no contest tomorrow, Jimmy. He isn't pleading guilty, he's pleading no contest. So all they can go off is what your girl says. And if
what she's saying is not true, then God help her. But if what she's
saying is true, then I want you to accept an apology on my behalf.

JIMMY   Ok.

COOPER   And I anticipate that this won't affect the deal you set up
between me and your father. The elongated enrollment thing.

JIMMY   That's why you called me.

COOPER   No.

JIMMY   You selfish, classless fuck.

COOPER   No. No no, I wanted to tell you. I wanted to clear the air
with—

JIMMY   How about, I'm sorry Jimmy. How about Jimmy do you need
anything? I'm so sorry man. I'm so sorry for you. Nope. None of
that—just good old Cooper. Watching out for himself.

COOPER   Honestly—

JIMMY   You're not in the clear, Coop. This is your house. That was your party. You pay rent here. You had your ear pressed against the door?

COOPER   No. Yes but—

JIMMY   And you did *nothing*?! (*Beat.*) You get off on that shit Cooper? Huh? You like that? You like it rough? I can play rough.

COOPER   I had nothing to do with any of it. Anything.

JIMMY   You were. You were it.

COOPER   I'm telling you.

JIMMY   We'll see.

COOPER   Jimmy—we play for the same team, you and me. I mean rugby, yeah. But in life. We see life as an ocean of options, we only want to take the ones that lead to happiness. I just want to be happy, man.

JIMMY   Be my guest. Be happy. But not on my campus.

COOPER   Wait.

JIMMY   Leigh's sister is waiting in the car.

COOPER   There was a girl here earlier, Jimmy. She saw Leigh after the party and she— (*Beat.*) Listen Jimmy—I don't date. (*Beat.*) I don't plan to. (*Beat.*) I don't have much about me that I enjoy. But being part of a team . . . feeling like you belong. This is rare. You and your dad need to know that I am not responsible and that I am not taking sides.

JIMMY   You had your ear . . . pressed . . . up against the door.

COOPER   I'm sorry.

JIMMY And what . . . did you hear. (*Beat.*)

COOPER I told you that—

JIMMY Cooper—I don't want you to lie. But I want to know whose side you're on. So what'd you hear?

COOPER I . . .

JIMMY We're just figuring out which side you're on.

COOPER Fine. I heard it.

JIMMY What?

COOPER I don't know. God, Jimmy. I don't know! What? What did I hear?

JIMMY Did you hear her scream?

COOPER Yes. I heard her scream. I heard her crying.

JIMMY Did she say anything?

COOPER Yes.

JIMMY What? What did she say?

COOPER She said no. She screamed no and I heard it.

COOPER *forces back his sudden emotion.*

COOPER God dammit. Fuck me.

JIMMY *goes to exit.*

So what? Am I good? Am I safe?

JIMMY You're fine. We play for the same team.

JIMMY *exits.* COOPER *is left alone.*

SCENE 8

The girls' apartment. It is morning. The room was left a mess. LEIGH*'s cell phone, sitting on the counter, rings. After a beat she enters from the bedroom. She answers the phone.*

LEIGH   Hey baby. Sorry I must not have heard it ring.

DAVIS *enters from the bedroom as well.* LEIGH *puts her hand up, indicating that he should not speak.*

LEIGH   No I know—Ok. Just honk. Ok. Ok. See you soon.

She hangs up.

DAVIS   What's going on?

LEIGH   Good morning.

DAVIS   Good morning.

LEIGH   Remember last night?

DAVIS   Very well.

LEIGH   Good. Do you want anything? Some breakfast? Cereal or some fruit or something?

DAVIS   No. I'm good.

DAVIS *lies on the couch, and as* LEIGH *starts getting dressed, we see multiple intense markings on her back.*

LEIGH   I have to say that last night was amazing.

DAVIS Really?

LEIGH Yeah. I don't think I've ever breathed that deep. I feel so good right now.

Beat. She waits for DAVIS *to weigh in. Nothing. He's not even looking at her. As she buttons her dress, she slowly waits for* DAVIS *to respond, but he's invested in his cell phone. She begins to realize that he is not going to say anything, and then, after losing hope—*

You need to leave though. Jimmy is on his way over.

DAVIS Oh Jesus. Ok.

DAVIS *gets dressed.* LEIGH *cleans up. They say nothing. After* DAVIS *is done, he starts to exit.*

DAVIS So—uh—later I guess.

LEIGH Ok. I'll see you at two.

DAVIS At two? (*Beat.*)

LEIGH What?

DAVIS We just—

LEIGH Yeah. (*Beat.*) You still—

DAVIS But.

LEIGH That hasn't changed.

DAVIS How could you do that with someone who— (*Beat.*) Are you kidding?

LEIGH Oh, God, you're so good at it.

DAVIS At what?

LEIGH Poor Davis.

DAVIS That's not who I am.

LEIGH Poor, sad Davis.

DAVIS That's not me, Leigh.

LEIGH No—I know. You're actually far more frightening.

DAVIS I am not.

LEIGH Have you talked to Natalie lately?

DAVIS What is sh— (*Beat.*) Leigh—listen to me. That was one time.

LEIGH Oh well first times don't count for you, I guess.

DAVIS She knew I didn't mean it.

LEIGH No. I'm sure it hurt your hand, too.

DAVIS I feel awful about that.

LEIGH Aww—

DAVIS Really. It killed me inside.

LEIGH Really? Really? That's good to know.

DAVIS Don't throw that in my face, do you hear me? That's none of your business.

LEIGH It tells me who I'm dealing with.

DAVIS I was drunk.

LEIGH I guess that's all it takes for you. I wish I had known there was a potential for bargaining before I went public.

DAVIS *That's* what this is about.

LEIGH You can keep your money.

DAVIS I don't have any.

LEIGH Well it looks like the tables are turning.

DAVIS You are such a leech.

LEIGH And they survive on blood. Key word: survive.

DAVIS You sure you wanna push me?

LEIGH I'm not afraid of you, Davis.

DAVIS *takes* GRACE*'s frying pan and swings it at* HALEY*'s bottle of wine, smashing it against the wall. He turns back to her and looks at her with silent strength and power.*

LEIGH Whoa! There it is. There's that rage. And you haven't even had a drink yet! No, Davis. I'm just a little smarter than I let off.

DAVIS Do you understand what you are doing to me? To my life?

LEIGH I'm taking logical steps to see to it that you are punished. Unlike Natalie, I prevail.

DAVIS Is this who you want to be Leigh? Of all the people you could be. Of all the options. This is what you decided on? Come on. Come on, Leigh! You're better than this.

LEIGH No.

DAVIS You know you are better than this.

LEIGH (*On the verge of angry tears.*) Why now? Tell me you fuck. Why now?

DAVIS You can be better than this, Leigh!

LEIGH Four years. Four years I was not good enough for you. And what makes me better than this? I will tell you, Davis. What makes me better than this is my future. The life that I can have. With Jimmy. With a protector and a provider and a man who can offer me four walls and a roof forever. (*Beat.*) I am choosing not to fall.

DAVIS Is that a confession?

LEIGH It is a promise. What happened happened. It happened, Davis. But my life is waiting. And it is exactly what I want. And you have actually helped me. This whole thing. This whole fucked up thing—is a blessing.

DAVIS Why?

LEIGH Jimmy can't save something that doesn't need to be saved. Look at me. The poor girl who is almost beautiful. And look what I'm about to have.

DAVIS I see nothing but a loser. Now and forever. Trash.

LEIGH I see possibility. Solutions.

DAVIS So you got your life all figured out, huh?

LEIGH I do.

DAVIS And what about me?

JIMMY *'s horn honks. He's in the driveway.* LEIGH *looks at the door and keeps her cool, trying not to panic.*

Beat.

LEIGH What about you, Davis?! What do you want from me? MORE?!

LEIGH *smacks herself hard across her face.*

DAVIS Bitch.

LEIGH More Davis?

LEIGH *rips her dress down the center.*

DAVIS BITCH!

LEIGH *messes up the apartment, throwing* GRACE*'s bull horn out of reach.*

LEIGH STOP DAVIS! OW STOP! YOU'RE HURTING ME!

She begins taking off her shoes.

DAVIS WHAT ARE YOU DOING? NO!

LEIGH NOW?!?!

DAVIS NO! NO!

DAVIS I SAID NO DAVIS! DO YOU REMEMBER MY TEARS ON MY FACE?

DAVIS No.

LEIGH MY CLIT ON YOUR SKIN?

DAVIS You want this!?

LEIGH DO YOU DAVIS?

DAVIS Do you?!

LEIGH DAVIS THE GO-[OD!]

DAVIS *grabs* LEIGH *by the throat. She struggles before* DAVIS *throws her onto the couch. She tries to get away, reaching for the door over the couch.*

LEIGH Jimmy!

DAVIS *grabs her. They struggle before* DAVIS *gets ahold of her and lies on top of her.* DAVIS *lifts up her skirt and pulls down her underwear.*

LEIGH Help!

He pulls down his own pants, holding LEIGH *in place. She tries one last time to get away.*

LEIGH SOMEBODY!

The lights go black. COOPER *appears in his own light. He is at rugby practice.*

COOPER Listen—we need stronger forwards. We ruined that line out, but this our chance. Zwicky, O'Neill, get the ball back!

Dark on COOPER. HALEY, *in a different light, appears.*

HALEY I'm so excited! I bought him Pomeranian food and Pomeranian toys. And baby, he already knows how to roll over. Watch!

Lights back up on LEIGH *and* DAVIS. *He penetrates.*

LEIGH NO!

Dark on LEIGH *and* DAVIS. JOHNSON *in his own light.*

JOHNSON I just wanted to say, this is the only place I wanted to work. I promise I won't let you down.

Dark on JOHNSON. JIMMY *in his own light.*

JIMMY We could put in a pool. And in a couple of years we can finish the basement. I think we found it. I think we found the one.

The lighting shifts to light the house, as we see DAVIS *and* LEIGH *recovering from the event.*

GRACE (*To the audience.*) And so, future leaders, what we have learned is with persistence, grace, a plan of attack, and that secret weapon of ours—healthy selfishness—we can accomplish any feat. We can acquire any goods. And we can get exactly what we want.

DAVIS Oh fuck. Oh God.

GRACE *turns back to the stage.* DAVIS *is pulling up his pants.* DAVIS, *weak and emotionally drained, then drops to his knees.* LEIGH *walks downstage center, worn and ruined.*

LEIGH (*Facing the audience.*) It's perfect, Jimmy. Thank you. It's just what I always wanted.

JIMMY *and* LEIGH *look at each other. They've made it.*

COOPER, HALEY, GRACE, JOHNSON, *and* JIMMY *appear in their lights.* GRACE *walks toward the stage, applauding. She turns back around, to face the audience. Once she finishes clapping—*

GRACE Really.

Blackout.